# IS THIS A HOUSE FOR HERMIT CRAB?

## MEGAN McDONALD

### Pictures by
### KATHERINE TILLOTSON

**NEAL PORTER BOOKS**
HOLIDAY HOUSE / NEW YORK

*Dedicated to the memory of Dick Jackson, our first editor,*
*and for Neal Porter, who guided Hermit Crab to a new home*

*—M.M. and K.T.*

Neal Porter Books

Text copyright © 1990, 2024 by Megan McDonald

Illustrations copyright © 2024 by Katherine Tillotson

All Rights Reserved

HOLIDAY HOUSE is registered in the U.S. Patent and Trademark Office.

Printed and bound in October 2023 at C&C Offset, Shenzhen, China.

The artwork for this book was created with watercolor, acrylic, finger paint, and collage.

Book design by Jennifer Browne

www.holidayhouse.com

First Edition

10   9   8   7   6   5   4   3   2   1

Library of Congress Cataloging-in-Publication Data

Names: McDonald, Megan, author. | Tillotson, Katherine, illustrator.

Title: Is this a house for hermit crab? / Megan McDonald ; pictures by
   Katherine Tillotson.

Description: First edition. | New York : Neal Porter Books / Holiday House,
   2024. | Originally published: New York : Orchard Books, ©1990 with
   illustrations by S.D. Schindler. | Includes bibliographical references.
   | Audience: Ages 4–8 | Audience: Grades K–1 | Summary: "A hermit crab in
   need of a new, bigger shell explores the beach, trying on a variety of
   unsuitable objects before finding the right fit"— Provided by
   publisher.

Identifiers: LCCN 2023007477 | ISBN 9780823452194 (hardcover)

Subjects: LCSH: Hermit crabs—Juvenile literature.

Classification: LCC QL444.M33 M34 2024 | DDC 595.3/844—dc23/eng/20230314

LC record available at https://lccn.loc.gov/2023007477


ISBN: 978-0-8234-5219-4  (hardcover)

Hermit Crab
was growing too big
for the house on his back.

It was time to find a new house. He crawled up
out of the water looking for something to
hide in, where he would be safe
from the porcupine fish.

He stepped along the shore,
  by the sea, in the sand . . .

scritch-scratch, scritch-scratch

. . . until he came to a rock.
Is this a house for Hermit Crab?
Turning himself around, Hermit Crab
backed his hind legs beneath it.
The rock would not budge.

It was too heavy.

So he stepped along the shore,
by the sea, in the sand . . .

scritch-scratch, scritch-scratch

. . . until he came to a rusty old tin can.
Is this a house for Hermit Crab?

When he tried to walk with the can
on his back, it bumped and clunked.

It was too noisy.

So he stepped along the shore,
by the sea, in the sand . . .

scritch-scratch, scritch-scratch

. . . until he came to a piece of driftwood.
Is this a house for Hermit Crab?

Hermit Crab crawled deep inside
the rounded hollow at one end.

It was too dark.

So he stepped along the shore,
by the sea, in the sand . . .

scritch-scratch, scritch-scratch

. . . until he came to a small plastic pail.

Is this a house for Hermit Crab?
Climbing up toward the rim—*oops!*—
he fell right in. He clawed,
and he clawed,
until he climbed back out.

It was too deep.

So he stepped along the shore,
by the sea, in the sand . . .

scritch-scratch, scritch-scratch

. . . until he came to a nice round hole in the sand.
Is this a house for Hermit Crab?

He poked his head down into the opening. A huge
pair of eyes blinked back at him. Hermit Crab
shivered as he scurried away from the big
fiddler crab peering out of its burrow.

It was too crowded.

So he stepped along the shore,
by the sea, in the sand ...

scritch-scratch, scritch-scratch

. . . until he came to a fishing net.

Is this a house for Hermit Crab?
When he poked his claws into the
heap, they got tangled and caught.
Hermit Crab wiggled and wriggled

until he found his way out of the net.
It had too many holes.

So he stepped along the shore,
by the sea, in the sand . . .

scritch-scratch, scritch-scratch

All of a sudden a gigantic wave tossed and tumbled
pebbles and sand over Hermit Crab's head.

He *swirled*

and whirled with the tide

and was washed back out to sea.

Sleeker than a shark, the prickly porcupine fish
darted out from its hiding place in the tall seaweed.
Mouth open wide, it headed right for Hermit Crab.

Hermit Crab raced across the ocean floor . . .

scritch-scritch-scritch-scritch-scritch

. . . scurrying behind the first creature he saw.

It was a sea snail, and he
hoped it would hide him,
but the shell was empty.

The shell was empty!

Hermit Crab scrambled inside as quick as a flash and clamped his claw over the opening in the shell.

The porcupine fish circled the snail shell three times, but it could not catch sight of the crab it had been chasing. It glided off in search of something else to eat.

When all seemed still and quiet, Hermit Crab snuggled comfortably down into his new shell. It was not too heavy, not too noisy, not too dark, and not too deep. It was not too crowded and it did not have too many holes.

At last Hermit Crab had found a new home.

And it fit just right.

# A Note from the Author

I first became fascinated with hermit crabs when my family vacationed on the Outer Banks of North Carolina. After visiting a local pet shop, I brought home my very own pet hermit crab. The next day I went to check on my pet in its tank, and guess what? It was gone! How had it escaped? I searched the house, but failed to find my new pet anywhere. Later that day, I went to put on my sneakers and found my pet hermit crab hiding out inside my shoe! *Youch!*

This childhood experience inspired me as a young writer to pen my *very first* picture book over thirty years ago—about a hermit crab trying out various "houses" in an effort to find the just-right home. A whole new generation of readers can now *scritch-scratch* along with Hermit Crab, brought back to life with newly imagined vibrant illustrations by the artist Katherine Tillotson. I'm grateful that after these many years, that first book, so near and dear to my heart, has found a new home with Neal Porter at Holiday House. And it fits just right.

# MORE ABOUT HERMIT CRABS

### Meet the hermit crab

A hermit crab is a **crustacean,** an aquatic animal that has a hard shell, ten jointed legs, and a segmented body. Hermit crabs live in waters all over the world, from the Atlantic, Pacific, and Indian oceans to the tropical Caribbean Sea and the Gulf of Mexico. But if you've ever had a pet hermit crab, it was most likely a land hermit crab.

   Unlike most crabs, hermit crabs can't grow their own shells. Instead, they "borrow" abandoned shells from other creatures for protection, like snails, whelks, and periwinkles.

### Hundreds of hermits

Scientists estimate that there are between 800–1,100 different kinds of hermit crabs. They can be as small as a thumbnail or as large as a coconut. The name "hermit" makes them sound like solitary critters, but hermit crabs actually have tons of friends. They like to hang out in groups of a hundred or more.

### True or false?

The hermit crab, unlike the blue crab or fiddler crab, is not a "true" crab because it has a softer body and can't grow its own shell. But this "false" crab has plenty of crustacean cousins, such as lobsters, crayfish, shrimp, and even pill bugs.

### That's a lotta legs!

One, two, three, four, *five*! That's how many pairs of legs can be found on a hermit crab, including a pair of claws. This **decapod** uses its claws for eating and defense. The second and third pair of legs are used for walking. The last two pairs of legs help the hermit crab move into and out of its shell. They also have two pairs of antennae. One pair of antennae acts as feelers, while the other is for smelling and tasting.

### Pinch me

Hermit crabs have one large claw and one smaller claw. The large claw is used mainly for defense—it can cleverly seal off the opening in the hermit crab's shell. The small claw is used for feeding and scooping up water.

### Two claws up!

Who doesn't like a good scavenger hunt? Hermit crabs are scavenger hunters forever searching for food. They eat whatever they can get their claws on—bits of mussels, crabs, and dead fish, teeny-tiny algae and stinky seaweed, and even detritus (e.g. poop!).

### Mobile home

Throughout their lives, hermit crabs change shells. A hermit crab isn't born with a shell on its back. So, it goes off in search of a cast-off shell from another creature for protection. As the hermit crab grows, it outgrows its adopted shell, and has to find a new, bigger shell. In some cases, hermit crabs may fight—*pow!*—over the same shell.

### Try this on for size

When an empty shell turns up on the beach, hermit crabs have been known to line up in order, biggest to smallest, to try on the new shell and see if it fits. The first crab's shell then becomes the new hand-me-down home, all the way down the line, a bit like a game of musical chairs. *Yikes!* The last one left may find itself without a shell.

### Friends for life

Hermit crabs share a special friendship with sea anemones. It's called a **symbiotic** relationship. They're partners! The sea anemone hitches a free ride on the hermit crab's shell, helping to protect the hermit crab with its stinging tentacles. In exchange, the sea anemone gets to eat lots of leftovers—bits of food that the hermit crab leaves behind.

## Trash talk

**Plastic pollution** is a real concern in our oceans. Plastic trash poses a big problem for hermit crabs. They might mistake a plastic bottle or cap or container for a new home.

Hundreds of thousands of hermit crabs die each year from getting trapped in plastic litter and debris. Beach cleanup volunteers who pick up plastic litter are not only helping the beauty of the beach—they may be saving a hermit crab's life.

## Porcupine? Pine cone? Pincushion?

No, it's a **porcupine fish**! Instead of scales, the porcupine fish has spines all over its body. When a predator swims too close, the porcupine fish will take in water and puff itself up until its spines stick out like a prickly pincushion. Because it has such strong teeth, snails, sea urchins, and hermit crabs make for a yummy treat.

## Fit as a fiddle

Fiddler crabs are **intertidal** creatures that live in mangrove forests, tidal creeks, sandbars, and along shorelines. This means they can survive being above water at low tide and underwater at high tide. Each fiddler has its own burrow. The burrow is a good place to hide from predators and retreat during high tides. At low tide, fiddler crabs are active. They can be seen feeding, fighting, drumming, waving, or "housecleaning"—tidying up their burrows. Male fiddler crabs have one large claw for fighting and one small claw for eating.

## How to find a hermit crab

Finding a hermit crab in its natural habitat can be a bit like going on a treasure hunt. Head for the ocean and find a rocky beach. Hermit crabs like to hide under rocks. Wait for it! Low tide, that is. Peer into a tide pool, where hermit crabs like to hang out when the tide goes out. Gently reach in and lift up a stone. A favorite shell of tide-pool hermit crabs is the black turban snail. So if you happen to spot a snail shell that takes off quickly on legs and scrambles to hide, it's probably a hermit crab.

**Eager to learn more about hermit crabs?** Here are a few resources to help you investigate.

**BBC Earth Kids video**
Can you say *conga*? Watch hermit crabs in action as they line up to exchange shells.
https://youtu.be/zpjklLt1qWk

**PBS Kids, Wild Kratts: Shell Surprise video**
Want to get up close and personal with a hermit crab? Follow the Wild Kratts as they introduce you to this curious crustacean.
https://www.youtube.com/watch?v=winbjiOI7YM

**National Geographic**
Learn about hermit crabs with stunning photos. Make sure to watch hermit crabs risk their lives for a tulip snail shell in the breathtaking "Hermit Crab vs. Horse Conch" video.
https://www.nationalgeographic.com/animals/invertebrates/facts/hermit-crabs

**California Academy of Sciences**
Make an egg-carton hermit crab and get colorful with the Tide-pool Coloring Sheet.
https://www.calacademy.org/search?gq=hermit+crabs

Special thanks to the following for research assistance and an up-close and personal peek at tide pools:

California Academy of Sciences:
Luiz A. Rocha, PhD, Curator and Follett Chair of Ichthyology and Dave Catania, Sr. Collections Manager, Ichthyology

UC Davis Bodega Marine Laboratory:
Molly Engelbrecht, MLIS, Laboratory Librarian, Cadet Hand Library

Monterey Bay Aquarium